BRAD,
Stay true to self.
Enjoy every day.
Love Cheyenne
Light

# Clarity
# Wisdom
# Harmony

Simple and Concise Tools for Living

By
Cheyenne R. Mease

SO-BIH-266

ALSO BY CHEYENNE
*Being In the Moment (cd)*
*Evelyn's Way (cd)*

Copyright © 2011 by Cheyenne R. Mease
www.CheyenneMease.com
610.346.9566

All rights reserved.
ISBN-10: 0615543529
ISBN-13: 978-0615543529
Second Printing

Edited by Brenda Lange
Cover design by Chanin Milnazik, BrownDogDesign
Photography by Terree Yeagle, The Moment Photography

Published by Autumn Productions

## DEDICATED TO

. . . my dear friend, Lisa O'Connell, who, after enjoying dinner with her family in July of 2009, left to make a quick run for coffee with all good intentions of seeing them again. A fatal car accident took her life that night at the age of thirty-eight, leaving her family and friends with a deep sense of loss and only memories to fill the void.

Not a day goes by when I am not reminded that life is precious, and whether we like to admit it or not, we all have one thing in common: we have one minute at a time. For none of us really knows when we will breathe our last breath, share our last smile, or give our last hug to someone we love.

# CONTENTS

# FOREWORD

Cheyenne's book contains the wisdom of the sages. These are age-old lessons that teach us how to survive and thrive. They provide us with what I call survival behavior. One does not need to become strong at the broken places when the experience and lessons of others are available to us. Just as her name, Cheyenne, came from a deeper place of conscious wisdom, so can this change and resource become available to you. Many years ago, in a dream, I was given the name Satchidananda. I learned from someone that it meant being, consciousness and bliss. This book can help you to achieve all those things and more.

With acceptance comes an inner peace. One's life is no longer about waging a war and empowering one's enemy but about finding peace, love and healing. The acceptance and surrender are not about giving up but about no longer battling and about learning from one's troubles and afflictions. Hunger leads us to find nourishment and so do our problems if we interpret them correctly.

When we do that we find true joy because when you have enough you do not need or desire anything more. Our consciousness knows how to prepare our future and when we have faith in ourselves and our future we create the path we were meant to travel. Life is always a journey and the resources for the trip are within us all. Cheyenne's words can help you to bring them forth.

So read on and let your heart make up your mind. When you do you will find a quiet mind, which like the still pond, free of turbulence, will allow you to see your true self and live your authentic life.

Bernie Siegel, MD
Author of *Faith, Hope & Healing* and *A Book of Miracles*

# Life Happened – Cheyenne's Story

Who am I? I am a daughter, a wife, a mother, a friend, a teacher, a speaker, and, to some, a healer. However, I realize these descriptions are simply labels.

Perhaps where I have been will give you more of an idea of who I am and why I wrote this book.

As a child, I can remember living with fear and worry. For some reason, I viewed life as a glass that was half empty. At the age of sixteen, a serious head injury from a motorcycle accident compounded my inability to experience joy. By the time I was seventeen, emotional and physical pain were my constant companions.

I never felt like I fit in somehow, and taking the accelerated track seemed like an answer to my prayers, allowing me to graduate high school in my junior year.

Even at this time, I realized I had a calling, if you will. I wasn't clear by any means what that was, I just knew that I had some type of journey ahead of me. My purpose in life was yet to be determined.

Recalling one of the happiest times of my life, when I was a young girl in love and engaged to my childhood sweetheart, I still felt unsettled. I can remember it like it was yesterday, taking off the engagement ring and saying, "Get out while you can." Imagine how hard it was telling the love of my life that I had some sort of roller coaster ride ahead of me and yet loving him enough to give him a chance to get out while he still could. He chose to hang in there, and at eighteen we were married.

One year later, expecting our first child, we were devastated by the loss of the baby. Within the next year, while we were building our first home, I found I was pregnant again with our son, Nevada. Twenty-two months later, I gave birth to our daughter, Cody. It was during that time my husband decided to quit his full-time job and begin his own excavation business.

Suffering from depression due to my head injury as well as caring for two babies, compounded by postpartum depression and hormonal imbalances, I felt my life was unbearable. The everyday events of life continued to pile up. At times, I believed that my absence would be easier for my loved ones. I struggled with the hopelessly sad person I had become. I admit, thoughts of ending it all ran through my mind.

I am grateful the angels heard my cry of despair. A friend of the family shared her story with me, beginning with her mother's suicide and ending with the way it had deeply affected so many individuals. The sad story helped me realize that I had to find a way to believe in myself and be a positive, supportive presence in my children's lives. It truly had been darkest just before the dawn.

Committed to changing my life, I read every self-help book that I could get my hands on and attended any and all parenting classes with the hope of being the best parent I could be.

I enrolled in photography classes at the local community

college because I loved the medium, which in time turned into a part-time business. I also worked part-time at a doctor's office for extra income and volunteered at a local hospital one day a week just to get out of the house. Drawn to helping others, I signed on as a volunteer for NOVA, Network of Victim Assistance, and trained to be a volunteer on the hotline. This opened the door to my next part-time, paid position as a presenter, teaching NOVA's "Be Safe" programs in the surrounding school districts.

Plus, I was still involved with our church and my children's school at times, which was like a part-time job without the paycheck. I was a soccer mom to two children plus one (my husband), attended numerous practices plus games, and then figured out how to work my life around it all. The part-time photography business was growing. During this time, I continued to support my husband in his business.

Right there at the top of the list with my husband and children were the needs of extended family and friends. Life was like a snowball rolling down a hill. My head spins just recalling all of it.

The realization that I was continually putting my SELF aside in favor of something or someone else began to haunt me. The everyday demands over the years had stepped down from the emotional level to the physical plane, my body had manifested everything from digestion issues to headaches. I woke up in pain and went to bed in pain. The medical community offered medications, which helped treat the symptoms.

Looking to heal the root cause of my pain, I turned to complementary therapies, or alternative healing, to support myself. The healing arts offered many new options. Utilizing several complementary therapies over time, the mind, body, and spirit found its way to a healthier state of being.

Since then I've been drawn to the healing arts. A friend suggested that I take a Polarity Therapy training course developed by Dr. Randolph Stone (1890-1981), who conducted a thorough investigation of energy in the healing arts over the course of his sixty-year medical career. His comprehensive exploration of the different dimensions of the human condition (physical, mental, and emotional) made it a fit for me. I began the first of many classes.

Always focused on being the best wife and mother possible, I was challenged at times to embrace my newfound passion. I knew in my heart that I needed to focus more attention and energy on my studies. With only so many minutes in a day and days in a week, I resigned from all volunteer positions, closed the photography business, and, when appropriate, said "no" to others, creating space in my life.

After commuting to New York City over several years for the bulk of my training, the day finally came for graduation, and I was certified as a Registered Polarity Practitioner and Educator, an accomplishment that affected my whole being at all levels. I was on track, knowing that my purpose was to work with the "traditional" medical community to help bridge the gap between conventional and holistic medicine.

Shortly after graduation, I contacted a physician about renting space in his building. Fortunately for me, he understood and respected the values inherent in complementary healing. Before

I knew it, physician referrals had me working with clients of all ages and developmental stages with a variety of life challenges. Inspired, I went on to study Bowen Theory in Princeton, New Jersey, enhancing the verbal portion of my work as well as gaining a deeper understanding of family dynamics.

Eight years into my private practice, it was time for a change. As a result, I closed my office in New Jersey and moved the practice into our home in Pennsylvania. Referrals from physicians continued to provide the majority of my client base.

Life continued to present challenges as it does for many of us. With both children off to college, I made a decision to make room for my husband's dream—owning a farm. Wishing doesn't make it happen. So, we had to sell our home and move into a rented house for more than two years, with most of our things packed in boxes. I quickly learned how to do with less and began the non-attachment phase of my life.

In the midst of it all, while giving my husband a polarity session, I discovered a lump on his neck and sensed it was cancer. He was officially diagnosed a month later with papillary thyroid cancer. Thankfully, his surgery, combined with complementary therapies, went well and he is cancer-free today.

Two years later, the opportunity to purchase his family's farm became our reality. The emotional drama of dealing with the extended family dynamics, the physical demands on the body, moving again, and the renovations of the farmhouse brought me to another challenging stage in life.

We had opened ourselves up to financial debt at a whole new level: the renovation of a two-family 1800s farmhouse, sixteen outbuildings, on seventy-plus acres all in need of love and attention. Doing everything we could to keep the family farm intact, I continued my private practice, while my husband Jeff, and son Nevada, continued to do excavation work along with farming an additional 700 acres and raising all-natural beef.

Out of the need to stay sane, patience, tolerance, and trust became my daily mantra.

At the same time, there was a need for a different thought pattern followed by a new action. You see, it has always been the simple ways of thinking and doing that have gotten me through some of the most difficult times in my life. Respecting myself enough to get clear about what was important to me, staying true to myself, and then articulating to others with respect was important for self-preservation.

Coming into the present moment, this strategy is not just for self-preservation, it has become the gateway to having joy in my life as I never knew it in the past.

I shared the practical wisdom I had applied to my own life with clients over the years and found it was successful for them. It became clear to me to write this book; simple metaphors that can be utilized by others in numerous ways to deal with the everyday events of life.

# Live the Life You Want

During my polarity studies, we were asked to write our obituaries. You can imagine my reaction to this assignment. Why would anyone in their right mind want to spend time writing about their life as if they were already dead? This was truly a stretch for me.

The first time, I found it to be a strange concept and even a bit uncomfortable, to say the least, the process of looking at life from the point of view that it's over. The realization that there is no chance to go back, to do anything more, or to do it differently is an amazing catalyst for making life-altering changes now.

Some years later, taking this way of thinking a bit further in a conversation with my husband, we explored the question, "If we had only a year to live, what would we do with it?" This discussion changed our lives forever.

He shared his desire to own and live on a farm with a purpose of caring for animals and raising crops. The dream came true with the purchase the farm.

During that profound conversation, I said I would stop worrying. I had realized that for most of my life I was a worrier, and I realized that most of the things I worried about on a regular basis were beyond my control. I knew that if I were to die that day, or even in a year, none of it would matter anyway. So in that moment, I chose to stop the worry. Yes, right there and then, I made a choice.

The saying, "If you are going to worry why pray, and if you are going to pray, why worry," was a good fit. Sometimes old habits die hard, so I found that if I was really struggling, I would light a white candle and say a prayer, rather than worry.

An opportunity came for me to apply this method when our daughter, Cody, announced she and three close girl friends would be taking their own high school senior trip to Mexico. Reminding myself that worry was not an option, I chose prayer.

I placed a white candle next to her graduation photo, lighting it every day while saying a prayer or sending out an intention such as, "May the girls have a safe, fun time in Mexico," kept me from worrying when she was away.

Another way to deal with the negative thinking or worry— you know, the thoughts that can jump right in our mind without notice—is to replace the statement or thinking with two positive statements or thoughts.

For example, if I was thinking something negative such as, "The girls might get hurt or it might not be safe," I first needed to recognize the negative thinking and then make the conscious choice to stop and replace the thought with two positive statements. Such as, "The girls are having a safe and wonderful time. I am certain the girls are safe and enjoying their vacation."

The other realization I had during that conversation was how deep my desire was to take the name Cheyenne—which was given to me in a powerful and spiritual dream several years before. This wasn't really a surprise to either of us, because I had discussed changing my name with Jeff in the past. However, I hadn't pursued it because I was concerned about how my loved ones might respond. The last thing I wanted to do was hurt my parents or embarrass my children. You see, not having been born in a culture where one is given a new name as a right of passage was a foreign concept in our part of the world and to my family of origin.

I was anxious that my parents might take it personally or not be supportive of me replacing my given name, Sherry Ann, with Cheyenne and taking back my maiden name, Roberson, to replace my middle name. There had been so much struggle and pain in my life that just the idea of taking this new name was like a breath of fresh air, a new beginning. It was something that meant so much to me, and I was passionate about it.

Still, the name change remained an issue. In my mind, it simply was not an option. For several years, every time I meditated, I would hear the same directive, "Take the name legally." My inner reply was always, "No, I can't do that."

Stepping out of my comfort zone was not easy. There was a deep fear of possible judgment from others as I chose to support myself. The nagging question remained, "What if my family and friends don't understand and choose to somehow take it personally?"

Jeff listened to me that day as we rode in the car, talking about what we would do if we had only a year to live and what was important for us. Even if he could not totally understand the importance, he heard me and embraced me that day with loving support to take the name Cheyenne legally.

This exercise truly was my wake-up call. The idea that life is to be lived in the now, because it can be over in a moment, was the catalyst to make the change. I hired an attorney and the rest is history.

Over the years, I have continued to utilize this exercise from time to time. It may be when I feel a bit stuck or just want to pause and redirect my life.

Many of my clients have used this process as well, and it has changed the way they think about their lives. The exercise has a way of moving you forward, keeping you on track to live life to the fullest with no regrets.

### *Writing Your Obituary*

The best way for me to do this process is to sit down with a pen and pad. Begin with a simple list of subtopics, such as your accomplishments in life and relationships with others. For example, your family, friends, co-workers, education, hobbies, career, you get the idea.

Now take it a step further and think about what others might say about you. Are you friendly, sad, happy, easy to be with, or do you make things difficult? Is it always about you? Are you a victim or maybe the sacrificial lamb in many situations in your life? Perhaps you are the hero, always saving everyone. This process is for your eyes only. Be honest with yourself and write it down.

Keep in mind that the whole idea is to learn from your writing. So when you've finished writing about your life, pause for a moment and reflect on how your obituary might read. Maybe put it away for a day or so and come back to it. Now do the best you can to write a few paragraphs about yourself and your life as it would read in the obituary section in the daily newspaper.

After reading what you wrote, it is important to take the time to reflect on it.

Then ask yourself these questions: If I were to die today, am I living the life I want? Am I being the person I want to be? Is this the way I wish to be remembered?

If you read your obituary and it doesn't reflect what you want it to, the way you wish to live and would hope to be remembered, then I suggest you begin right here, right now. Go ahead; if I can do it, you can do it. If you need help, find someone to support you in making those changes.

Even if you make only one small change, to quote Nike, "Just Do It!"

It's never too late to live your life with joy in your heart, in the now, being the person you want to be.

### *Note to Self*

We all have one thing in common; we live one minute at a time. For none of us really knows when we will breathe our last breath.

# Master of My Fate
## Captain of My Soul

The famous line from the poem *Invictus,* written by William Ernest Henley in 1875, "I am the master of my fate: the captain of my soul," found its way into my life on a greeting card given to me at a retreat many years ago.

Moved by the quotation, I framed the card as a daily reminder with the hope that it might be a silent message for my children, and I placed it on the bathroom counter.

The concept of being the captain of my own life and master of my soul seemed unattainable at that time. I was uncomfortable in my own skin for so many years, in fear that others would not respect, love, or include me in their lives if I showed who I was on the inside. Simply giving myself permission to quietly explore the idea of having a different viewpoint than those around me was a risk; one I had not been able to take.

I knew that defining "self" was an important part of being the master of my own fate, the captain of my soul, and I had to be true to myself. However, the idea of stating my opinion when different from others on social, political, sexual, and religious beliefs, not to mention career and social activities, was difficult.

I struggled with the issue of being true to self, especially when I found I did not agree with a belief system that others held. Somehow, I felt it was being judgmental, taking a different position than theirs, making myself right and them wrong.

Being judgmental was never a trait I aspired to in my life, and the conflict within me continued to be a challenge. Not to mention there was also the dreaded fear of being judged and therefore no longer accepted by the group. The need to belong, to be loved and accepted, held me hostage.

Often, in meditation, I reflected on the conflict within myself, how to be true to my own beliefs and not judge others, side by side with the fear I carried of being judged and rejected.

One day, the word "discernment" came to me. I wasn't totally sure what that meant in relationship to being true to myself, not judging or being judged, and so, as I often do when a word is given to me in meditation, I referred to the dictionary.

According to *Webster's New Compact Desk Dictionary* - Discern: verb. to perceive or recognize clearly. Discerning: adj. having good judgment; astute.

Being judgmental does not allow for growth, but discernment gives way to having good judgment. Many people have never even considered accepting others who are different.

Discernment helps to respect another's belief system and recognize that they're not necessarily right or wrong. They simply hold a different viewpoint. Discernment supports you in being in unconditional love regardless of the actions and beliefs of others.

We can step back and take a good, long look at what is happening, get the clarity needed either to stay with an old belief system or shift to a new one. This requires respecting self as well as others. When we cannot see both sides of an issue, we must allow for the differences rather than judging. The ability to accept with unconditional love promotes a new level of tolerance for those who differ from us.

The freedom to observe self and others without judgment, using discernment, allows you to get clear as to whether a particular belief or action is or is not something you are okay with in your life. You do not give up self; rather, you are being true to yourself.

It wasn't until years later that I read the poem in its entirety and realized how much the words spoke to the depth of my being. You never really know when Spirit will bring you the wisdom you need in your life. A few simple lines on a greeting card changed the course of my life forever and, I suspect, may have been a sound influence in my children's lives as well.

You are just as worthy as any other person to be who you are and believe what you believe. For those individuals or groups who are no longer a fit for you or you for them, remember that when one door closes another one opens, making room for others to come into your life. So practice unconditional love and be true to yourself.

Ultimately, you will attain a new level of contentment and peace of mind that will stay with you even if you are told that your way is wrong.

It is okay to be the master of your fate and the captain of your soul.

### Action
1. Choose a quote or poem that inspires you, perhaps one you want to share with loved ones.
2. Print it or write it out.

The simple act of putting a poem or quote framed on the wall or stuck on the refrigerator door is a way to remind yourself, as well as share with others without coming on too strong. You offer daily guidance to yourself and wisdom to others you love without being pushy.

# The Cavemen Ate Raw Meat

## Take Yourself Down Off The Whipping Post

Have you ever done something, and, as time goes by, upon reflection, you wonder why you did it? Do you find yourself feeling guilty—beating yourself up about it?

Rarely at the top of my list of things to do is to take the time to reflect on life, being totally honest about what worked and what didn't. I do find value in the process. However, if you are not careful, you can get stuck on an issue from the past, keeping yourself on the whipping post for something you did or didn't do in your life.

One simple example, or hotspot, for me was feeling badly that I had "messed up" by giving my children antibiotics in their formative years, rather than first trying a more holistic approach.

"What was I thinking, taking my children to a board-certified physician when they were sick?" I might ask myself, knowing what I do now about the benefits of complementary medicine.

I was raised in a family that believed in traditional Western medicine, and often an antibiotic would be my first course of action. Years later I learned of natural remedies as a possible first line of defense. New knowledge was something to be thankful for and celebrate.

I finally realized how crazy that sounded, having done nothing wrong by taking my children to the pediatrician, who often wrote a prescription for antibiotics. I simply did what I knew.

Think of the cavemen and women as they discovered fire for the first time and then began to integrate it into their lives. They never considered beating themselves up for eating uncooked meat when they didn't even have the concept of "cooking" yet!

They simply utilized this new knowledge and applied it to many areas of their lives.

It was time to get down off the mental whipping post once and for all. No more feeling guilty and beating myself up for the way things were done in the past.

Even someone who has been abused or who realizes a loved one has been victimized can use this exercise. If they find themselves self-blaming, saying, "If only I had done something different" it's time to forgive and realize they didn't have the necessary knowledge. Like the cavemen, they did the best they could with the tools they had at the time.

Build a fire and burn the whipping post. Make the choice to celebrate every time you find a new and supportive way to be in life.

### *Action*

1. Get a piece of paper.

2. Make a list of the things you regret, those things you think you should or could have done differently in the past for yourself or others. This is your whipping post and whip, your wood to burn. Get real and be totally honest with yourself as you make this list.

3. Now get rid of the paper—either burn it in a fireplace or outside fire pit. Otherwise, shred it in a paper shredder or rip it up into little pieces and put it in the trash can.

4. Take the time to feel the release in your body.

5. Repeat this process whenever needed.

# Staying on Track

Have you ever wondered why you do the things you do or make the choices you make?

Does it feel like you get off track or have too many irons in the fire, not sure which ones to let go and which ones to keep?

If you answered "yes," I suggest you try working with the following question. (I'm not sure where it originated, or even how it came to me, in order to give credit where credit is due.) It is simple and to the point.

"Does (action, thought, person, place) get me closer to or further away from (my life's goal or desire)?"

You might find it helpful to write out the question, leaving blank spaces to fill in the action, thought, person, or place you are considering. This would go in the first space. The second space would contain your life's goal or desire.

For example, some goals might be: happiness, good health, more time with the family and friends, financial stability, a college degree, change in career, good relationship, owning a home, peace of mind, etc.

It is always important to remember this is your life's goal, desire, or purpose, not what someone else thinks you should or should not do.

The first blank might be something as simple as eating a particular food, drinking a particular drink, smoking, or even thinking certain thoughts, or as complex as making a large purchase, being in a relationship, or living in a certain environment.

Or perhaps after reading the previous chapter, "Live the Life You Want," you might be thinking, "What now?" You may even be feeling stuck and not sure where to go from here.

I am grateful to have the process, applying it on a regular basis when there is a decision to make in my life on how I wish to use my time, energy, or money.

When there is a need for clarity, to make a choice that aligns with my highest good, I simply ask this question to keep myself on track. I have the question on my desk where I can read it daily.

You may wish to put this question on your PDA, laptop, date planner, checkbook, or even something as simple as a note on your refrigerator. Find a place you will read it on a regular basis to help keep you on track, living the life that is right for you, with no regrets.

### *Action*
1. Make a list of your goals, the things you desire in your life.
2. Take the time to write or print out the question. "Does _____ get me closer to or further away from _____?"
3. Fill in the blanks for each goal. This question can be used for as many different goals or desires as you wish.
4. Place it in an area where you can read it whenever you

need clarity on how you choose to give your time, energy, or money to someone or something. You can fill in only the second blank space with your goal and leave the first blank empty, in order to apply the questions to the actions at hand.

You will find clarity using this simple formula whenever needed. Trust me when I say that by staying on track, living the life that is best for you will become much easier.

### Note to Self
Remember to ask the question.

# Realizing the Power of Acceptance

As much as I might love Reinhold Niebuhr's famous *Serenity Prayer*, sometimes I find it frustrating and difficult to embrace. The idea of acceptance creates turmoil for some individuals.

For example, many of my clients, their family members, and/or close friends have been victims of physical, emotional, mental, and/or sexual abuse. The idea of acceptance in situations like these often presents a huge challenge and is compounded when a friend of the family or a relative has been the perpetrator.

For example, the first line, "God grant me the serenity to accept the things I cannot change," conjures up many emotions for some individuals.

Working with clients, I have found it can be a formidable concept—to *accept* in such situations.

We cannot change the past or change others; what happened, happened. All the wishing in the world will not make it go away.

However, some individuals lie awake at night going over and over it in their heads. They ask themselves unanswerable questions: Why did this happen? What could I have done differently? Am I a bad person? Was it my fault?

The desire to be validated and to have others see our purpose in the world can create an endless loop of thoughts in our minds. The idea of revenge can become an obsession, wanting the other person to feel the depth of hurt they have caused and feel some sense of remorse.

This way of thinking, even when justified, is like swallowing poison with the hope that the other person will die.

The questioning becomes less than supportive, taking time and energy from our everyday lives. Many of life's precious moments are absorbed in this pattern, rather than accepting the fact that there are things we cannot change.

It would be less painful to stick your head in the opening of a doorway (metaphorically speaking, of course) and slam the door a few times than to continue to ask the question "Why?" The fact is we will never really know the answer.

It is with passion that I express the idea, "You've got to get it between the ears!" By that I mean you have to "get it," internalize it, and recognize that you cannot change the past and, most importantly, that you are not likely to ever understand the "it."

So hold yourself accountable, and the minute you find you are in the "why-and-what-if" looping, stop thinking and jump into a new thought pattern that is more supportive. See this as an opportunity to refocus your thoughts and stop the outflow of energy that could otherwise be utilized to move you forward in life.

### *Acceptance At Its Best*

I have worked with so many individuals over the years who have experienced some sort of abuse—physical, mental, emotional, or sexual—and are struggling with letting go of the anger. For whatever reason, they have not been able to get beyond it.

They come to see me when they recognize that anger doesn't

support their lives.

At some point in our time together I will ask, "What did this experience teach you? What could you be thankful for? What is the gift or lesson?"

You can imagine the emotions any one of these questions might conjure up for someone who has had another person hurt them at such a deep and lasting level. You can imagine the reactions I get.

Even with the trust relationship we have established, this is a hard one for them to hear. The energy in the room often becomes very intense.

If the client is at a loss for answers, I suggest that most individuals who have a painful history such as theirs almost always reply, "I would never do that to another person, not even an enemy." If my clients are parents, they say, "I would never treat my child that way." It's at this moment that many receive the reassurance they long for and need, the knowing that they will not repeat the pattern. The fear that they could become their parent has been faced head on.

I simply point out that this is a gift. They know they will never hurt another the way they have been hurt.

It is important to understand that I am not suggesting anyone asks for or deserves to be abused. It is only after much prayer and meditation on why others are hurt so badly, often by those who are their caretakers and should be providing protection, support, and unconditional love, that the concept "nothing is good or bad" can be understood. I often say, "It just is." And that works for me. I believe if we can learn from what happened to us, we can move forward with joy in life. What was once a stumbling block becomes a stepping stone.

I have found this concept helps many loving beings find a way to get past the hurt and support themselves.

So I say, "Celebrate!" Your soul has learned a powerful lesson and there is no need to learn it again. Your heart is filled with love and compassion for others and knows that abuse is wrong. You can trust in knowing that you will never hurt another in this way. To take it a bit further, if someone begins to treat you in such a way you will remove yourself from the relationship. You are worthy of love and joy in your life.

Also very important is to take the time to be sad and mourn the loss of whatever that experience has taken, while being mindful of enjoying life every day. This is a chance to shift one's way of thinking.

Once clients wrap their brains around this concept, it is as if time has stopped and things are reorganizing. The energy in the room becomes very still. I can feel their peace. I can see the understanding in their eyes as they are finally able to be true to the person they are deep inside: a loving individual, no longer at war inside.

It has been said that knowledge is to know and wisdom is to do. Which is so beautifully stated in the essence of Niebuhr's *Serenity Prayer*, "having the serenity to accept things you cannot change, the courage to change the things you can, and the wisdom to know the difference."

The knowing is the gift and the wisdom is in the doing, the new thought pattern.

### *Action*

1. Write a letter filled with details, and really pour your heart and soul into it. Address it to the person who hurt you. Now read it out loud. Let yourself really feel it. Express yourself, and know that it's okay to be hurt or mad or whatever emotion you have.
2. Then give yourself permission to move past it and get on with living your life to the fullest.
3. Know that you can express your pain to the universe. Maybe you can burn the letter to let it go.

### *Note to Self*

Remember—it's better to love yourself and have joy in your life than to let the past rule the present.

## When My Ship Comes In

"When my ship comes in…my life will be easy…I will have joy in my life…"

How often have you heard this expression?

The ship in this case is everything you think you need or want. Note that the ship never seems to arrive; you're always waiting.

Oftentimes, what we need or want in life does not always show up the way we might expect. We can often manifest our desires, although sometimes they can show up in a very different form, only to be missed.

You already may have heard the following story; however, I feel it is worth repeating. (When I first heard this, the man was praying to God. Feel free to substitute whatever you hold as a higher power.)

*A man is sitting in his living room, watching TV and listening to the weather report. The meteorologist says that the rains are not going to let up and flooding is expected in the area. He advises everyone to take precautions. The man begins praying, "Please watch over my home and keep me safe."*

*The next day he hears voices from the loudspeaker of the fire truck as it makes its way down the street. "Please gather your belongings and make your way out to the highway as quickly as possible!" The man again prays, "Please watch over my home and keep me safe."*

*Now the river has begun to rise, and the water is in the street outside the man's home. He moves to the second floor. A rescue boat comes by and the crew does their best to talk him into getting in the boat, telling him he needs to go with them now. Choosing to stay, the man replies that he is praying and is sure he will be safe.*

*The water continues to rise, and he now must make his way to the rooftop. A helicopter flies over, and the voice on the loudspeaker instructs him to grab the rope. The man replies, "I have been praying. I will be safe." He chooses once again to stay, praying, "Please watch me, keep me safe."*

*Lastly, the waters continue to rise, he is swept away in the rush of the current and drowns.*

*Now, finding himself in Heaven, he says to God, "What happened? I prayed to you. I believed in you. I told everyone you would watch over me and keep me safe."*

*God replied, "I sent you a TV announcement. I sent you a fire truck with a last chance to drive out. I sent you a boat and rescue workers. And lastly, I sent you a helicopter and more brave individuals willing to risk their own lives for you. You chose not to accept any of them. It is your free will that has brought you here so soon."*

Simply by being open to different possibilities in life, you might find everything is not on a ship coming into the harbor. Rather, it has already arrived on a big, long, black train that is in the station just waiting for you to unload all life has to offer.

So remember that your "ship" isn't always what you think it might be.

### Action

1. Make a list of the things you have now.
2. Think of what you will do when your ship comes in.

# Happiness — Joy

What, you may ask, is the difference between happiness and joy?

The dictionary defines happiness as contentment.

"Happy" is defined as feeling satisfied that something is right, showing pleasure, contentment, or joy.

"Joy" is defined as feelings of great happiness or pleasure, often of a spiritual kind.

Many people experience happiness, as it can be a byproduct of relationships or new experiences. Some even buy happiness, in the form of a new car, boat, pair of shoes, or vacations.

We may feel happy when we are with loved ones, purchase something we want, or achieve a goal. However, that feeling can be lost very quickly if we are unable to continue to feed the need—for instance, if a relationship ends in separation, divorce, or death. Maybe we can't afford that new car we have grown accustomed to getting every year. These forms of happiness are almost an addiction. They are not self-sustaining.

Joy, however, is something that resides within us, and no person, place, or thing can produce it for us or take it from us.

So you might ask, "Where does joy come from?"

It's the embodiment of Spirit within one's self or the expression of such. Joy comes from unconditional love.

Being in or having unconditional love for self or another

means to look with the eyes of an innocent child, with no judgment or expectation—remembering that unconditional love is to have no preconceived ideas, conditions, no push or pull, right or wrong. It just is what it is.

Unconditional love equals joy.

### Action
1. Make a list of ways you express unconditional love.
2. Make a list of how you receive unconditional love in your life now.
3. List ways you can create or open yourself up to more unconditional love.

# Get a No? Let it Go!

The idea that material things, relationships, and emotions hold an energy that either support or drain was a new concept that came into my life just when I needed it.

I found it became necessary to let go of the things that no longer served me in order to make space for passion in my life.

Have you ever taken the time to ask yourself the question, "Do I love it or do I need it?"

Just ask yourself this simple question, without the drama, maybes, or I-don't-knows: Do I love it or do I need it?

It either serves you and your goals or it doesn't.

If you get a "no," let it go!

At times it can be just as simple as recycling old newspapers or as challenging as letting go of a draining relationship.

I found one way to get clarity was to think of everything in life as either dry wood that will feed the inner fire or wet wood that is not supportive.

Dry wood includes good relationships, a job that you love, hobbies that you are passionate about, and a living environment that is right for you.

Examples of wet wood would be people in your life who often seem to see the glass as half-empty, complaining about everything. Others might be individuals who do not respect you, those who take advantage of your time, money, energy, and loving heart.

The internal wet wood may be a repetitive thought pattern or negative emotion such as jealousy, hate, anger, or judgment, to name just a few.

Wet wood places might be spending too much time inside when you need to be outdoors enjoying nature. Some of us are country folks while others thrive in the city environment.

Your current lifestyle, job, career, and volunteer positions may not be supportive, hence wet wood.

Another example of wet wood includes material possessions you really do not love or need.

Saying "no" to wet wood provides more space for the dry wood to feed the inner fire, your passion in life, healthy relationships, and the time and energy to be with the people, places, and things you love.

### Action

1. Take a pen and pad and make a list of the things that no longer serve you.
2. Use a separate piece of paper for each area of your life. For example, at the top of each page put the headings:
   - Home
   - Office
   - Car
   - Personal Beliefs
   - Emotional Connections/Attachments
   - Friends
   - Family

Writing it down is helpful. It gives you direction. As you eliminate what is not supportive (wet wood) in your life, having something to check off can feel really good.

When doing the physical spaces (apartment, home, or office), begin first with a walkthrough. Stop and sit a minute and imagine you are seeing the space for the first time; notice your surroundings.

Simply ask yourself if there is anything in your space that is not pleasing to the eye.

Ask the questions: Do I need it? Do I love it? Does it serve a purpose in my life?

If you hear an internal "no" on two or more of these questions, then write that item down on your pad. There is no need to justify why it doesn't support you. It just doesn't.

This list will come in handy when you are finding a home for the items.

It is always easier to let something go if you know that someone else can use it. Feel the power of checking off the list as you remove those items from your life.

The list will become your map and guide to take the steps you need to create a life with only supportive, dry wood to feed the fire.

You can repeat the same steps for each heading.

For family and friends: You might want to sit quietly in the comfort of your home, or your list may come just as easily at lunch one day in a noisy café. Write down the name of each individual in your life. (I suggest skipping a line to give room for the next step.)

Keeping a running list as you experience someone in your daily life is another easy way to get everyone you interact with on the list.

It makes no difference, as long as you make the list.

Now go back and quickly look over the list. Next to a non-supportive person, write WW (wet wood), and next to supportive people in your life DW (dry wood).

Once you have your list finished, transfer the non-supportive names to another sheet of paper, leaving space between the names so you can write out any feelings they bring up for you that are not supportive—why they are wet wood and do not feed your inner fire.

This list can then be posted as a reminder to invest as little time with them as possible or find another way to deal with that individual. (See chapters "The Shredder" and "Be a Duck.") Once you have this list and are ready, you can either put it through a paper shredder or burn it. Always take a moment to give thanks for the lessons these individuals have given you. Oftentimes we learn as much, if not more, from the wet wood in our lives, especially when we are ready to let go, no longer giving others the power to influence us.

This exercise can be done more than once in your life. Some great days to use this process would be on your birthday, New Year's Day, the spring and fall equinox, or winter and summer solstice. You may find that utilizing this exercise on a regular basis will continue to feed your inner fire with little to no effort.

# The Shredder

Growing up we had a saying, "Sticks and stones will break my bones but words will never hurt me." Well, as my grandmother might have said, I beg to differ.

I don't know about you, but for me, when another child said something mean, perhaps making fun of me or saying nasty things to me, it hurt. Even now as an adult, with many different tools, mean words can still affect me.

I repeatedly remind myself, "No one can make me feel a certain way. I get to choose what I take in and what I don't." Use the concept of wet wood verses dry wood. However, it can still be difficult at times to not let the words hurt, especially at an emotional level.

Verbal abuse comes in all shapes and sizes. Often the most hurtful words come from a person you thought you could trust. They can come from those closest to us, such as our family and friends. When this happens, it is time to bring out the "shredder."

Many of us have a paper shredder in our home or office. You know what a shredder can do to a piece of paper, even a plastic credit card. I suggest that when someone is being mean, saying unkind words to or about you, that you picture a "shredder" in front of your heart, or even one at each ear. So when the words are spoken to you, simply push shred.

One of my clients, a mother of three girls, shared this concept of the shredder with her youngest daughter who was having an issue with a girlfriend in high school, saying mean things to her.

Later, when the daughter witnessed someone speaking to her mother in a harsh way, she reminded her mom to simply use the shredder and shred it. Both women found it to be a simple and useful way to handle words that might otherwise have hurt them in the past.

Miguel Ruiz, author of *The Four Agreements*, a book I highly recommend, states it well when he speaks of "not taking anything personally" and how it is all about the other person's projection.

### *Note to Self*
It's not always about you.

## Creating a Comfortable Seat

I often wonder why so many people are on the fence.
Is the grass really greener on the other side?

Time and time again I hear friends and clients talking about how unhappy they are with something or someone in their lives.

Life presents us with choices…in our relationships, careers, child rearing, and so on. Often we find ourselves stuck in the decision-making process and we don't know which way to go. I call this "being on the fence."

Why don't we get down and simply graze in another pasture? Well, for some, the pastures are not so easy to be in; they may be full of groundhog holes, manure, and sticker bushes. You get the point. It's just easier or safer to stay put.

Another reason for some to stay on the fence might be that by being held accountable or taking a stand on an issue, we risk being wrong.

No way. Anything but that! I can't be wrong.

The ego wants—needs—to be right as much as possible. We love to be loved.

The desire not to hurt another person can also keep us on the fence, in addition to other reasons such as fear of the unknown, lack of self-esteem, no sense of direction, or exhaustion. For some, it's just plain laziness.

So, rather than make a choice, pick a direction, or take a side, we sit on the fence.

Let's face it, when sitting on the fence, you are not fully present in your life, job, or relationships. It may seem safer on some level to hover rather than be present. However, it can get pretty uncomfortable with a post up your butt!

If this is something you can relate to, no matter how you got there or what your reason, I strongly suggest you create a comfortable seat with a good vantage point—a bird's eye view. Simply recognizing this provides a new level of clarity and a place from which to view your life in its present situation.

Allow yourself the opportunity to gain an understanding of how or why you are on the fence; give the gift of allowing yourself to be comfortable there while the Universe presents you with choices. Then you can call in the strength and wisdom to move down off the fence when the time is right.

Another option might be to just get down off the fence now rather than creating a seat. Become completely engaged in your life, relationships, and job now. Really tune in, feel what works and what does not. I offer you the phrase, "for now, just for now." You will find it becomes very clear if something is not supportive, if it is wet wood. Then when you get a "no," you can let it go, or, in this case, move on to greener pastures.

# Is It Good for Me?

Just because you are good at what you do, doesn't mean it is good for you.

For example, a client scheduled an appointment with me for support in making a life-changing decision. A position with much more responsibility had become available in her company, one that she always aspired to attain. Her co-workers encouraged her to apply. They felt she would be a plus to the company and, in the new position of authority, make their lives easier as well.

Working with her in session that day, I began to ask questions about the position: who, what, where, and why. Getting in a bit deeper, getting the feeling of it all, I asked about the group dynamics of this new job and the individuals she would be interacting with in the new position. Her reply came very quickly. She said one aspect of the new job required dealing with a difficult group on a daily basis, when currently, she only had to deal with them occasionally.

Exploring this issue a bit more, as the session came to an end, I suggested she ask herself if the new position would be good for her. We had already established that she would be great at it for a number of reasons. The real question here was, would this position be supportive and a good fit for her?

We scheduled her next appointment and said our goodbyes.

At the next session, my client came in glowing. She had gained amazing clarity on what to do. My question, "Is this good for you?" had struck a chord. Even with all her co-workers' encouragement, a raise in pay, and the fact that for many years this was a position she felt she wanted to be in some day, she realized it would not be supportive for her. Now knowing it would not be a comfortable fit, she decided happily not to apply.

When given the opportunity to make a change, it is important to take the time to see all aspects. Look at it from all sides. Like moving from one chair at the table to another, each seat will provide you a different perspective.

But beware. We have a tendency to see what we want to see and gravitate to what we know, as in what we are comfortable with, rather than looking at or experiencing the whole. This is when being in the moment and being totally honest with yourself is important. Something you wanted years ago may not be in your best interest today.

Ask yourself as many questions as possible to get the facts, not what you want it to be, rather what it really is, with the final questions being: Is this good for me in the now? Does this feed the inner fire?

Make sure it is dry wood and works for you.

### *Note to Self*
Always take the time to listen and then trust the answer.

# Sort the Laundry

How often in your everyday life do you find yourself in situations that seem overwhelming and you just don't know how to begin to deal with them?

To be honest, life's everyday events, the little things, can build up like a large pile of laundry. They continue to stack up slowly until one day you find yourself with a whole lot of items that call for your attention.

When that happens, I take inventory. I sort the piles. As I begin to sort out the whites from the darks and towels from the hand-washables, that overwhelming pile of dirty laundry becomes more manageable. The simplest for me are the towels, an easy load to do. I choose hot water, click on the extra wash setting and fill the machine with the dirty towels. The soap goes in, the lid goes down, the pile is smaller, and now I can look to the next load to be done.

To apply the idea of sorting the laundry to everyday life, make a list of all that life demands—responsibilities, commitments, everyday chores, career, goals, and desires.

### Action

1. Turn off the phone.
2. Create time and space, and get clarity.
3. Make a list.
4. Transfer each item from the list to an individual piece of paper.
5. Prioritize what is an immediate need and what can wait.
6. Take action, manifesting a supportive outcome in your life.

### Note to Self

You cannot do it all at once and do it well. Taking one pile at a time, it becomes doable.

# Scale of 1 to 10

Do you ever have trouble getting clarity in making a decision or find it difficult to communicate your needs to others?

If you get a "yes" to either of these questions, then the "Scale of 1 to 10" may be just what you need to simplify. It's a great way to get grounded, get factual, and stay out of the drama while deciding what's important in life.

The Scale of 1 to 10 is utilized in many ways. This exercise is a simple way of measuring the value of something. It is a simple and succinct tool to get focused and stay on track when making choices.

Using the Scale of 1 to 10 allows individuals to state their positions to self or others.

### Ask the questions:
1. How important is this _____?
2. How invested am I in the outcome of _____?

The number 1 when using the Scale of 1 to 10 means this is something that is not of interest and you don't wish to use your time or talents in this way.

The number 10 means it has a great deal of value and it is something you are passionate about in life. It's worthy of putting your time and energy into manifesting.

The number 5 would be the middle of the road. You could go in either direction with your decision or choice.

If you get less than 5, you may choose not to invest any time and energy. The number 6 or higher may be a go!

For example, when working with others, personally and/or professionally, there are often collective choices to be made about money, time, or energy, and how they will be spent. The Scale of 1 to 10 can be used to find common ground, keeping things factual and out of emotional drama, focusing on what is important rather than playing "Twenty Questions."

When dealing with others, you might find that taking an average may result in finding that common ground. For example, if one person says it's a 9 to them and the other one says they feel it's a 4, the average would be 6.5. So as a group, this may be worth the effort. Or if it's a couple, then the person who feels it's a 9 might choose to do it on their own instead of expecting or hoping their partner will join them, even though they gave it only a 4.

Simply ask the question, "On a Scale of 1 to 10 would I like to _____?" Then listen for the answer.

I repeat, listen to the answer and allow it to direct you.

Once you get the answer, be it from yourself or another, you can then move in a direction that is most supportive. You will either do it or not do it.

As I said, it is simple and direct.

So when you have to decide on how to spend your time, energy, or money on an event, project, even a vacation, whether you're alone or in a group, this strategy will help ensure you are doing what you want to do—not what you think you should do or what you think someone else wants you to do.

### *Note to Self*

The Scale of 1 to 10 works as long as you are ready to hear the truth. Remember, if you can't or don't want to hear "no," as in less than 5, you may have an attachment to the outcome and the Scale of 1 to 10 may not work for you in this situation.

# Clear the Mind Clutter

When my mind is on overload and all the clutter seems to get in the way of actually getting something done, I find it helpful to get it out of my head and down on paper. It makes the task of moving forward with clarity and without drama much easier. So if you can relate, get yourself a stack of blank index cards and a pen, and we can get going.

Before using this method, it will be useful for you to have read the chapters "Sort the Laundry" and "Scale of 1 to 10." These are similar tools that will provide you with more direction on how to prioritize needs and wants.

You can divide the tasks in your life into two categories: things you need to do—such as feed the dog, pay the bills, clean the house, or buy groceries—and things you want to do—such as go to the movies, call a friend, take a walk, or read a book.

On one index card, write "Things I Want to Do" and on another, write "Things I Need to Do."

Place each one of these index cards on the table in front of you.

Now write out a task or desire on individual cards, one card for each task. Feel free to make notes on the back of each card about who, what, where, why, and how. Allow this to be a place for brainstorming any and all details that might assist you in taking action to manifest the individual task on that card.

Ask yourself with each card, "Is this a want or a need?" Then place them under the appropriate heading (index card).

Once you have them under the heading that fits best, go ahead and arrange them in the order of importance, or desire, using the Scale of 1 to 10. Remember, you have freedom of choice within any situation. You are in charge even when it may not seem that way.

Slide your "need to do" cards together, the most important task—the one that has to be done first—at the top of the pile. For example, paying the bills if they are due soon and feeding the animals come first, while dusting or sweeping can wait. Now slide your "want to do" cards together in a separate pile. You will have the things you are most passionate about doing for yourself at the top of this pile.

I like to either put a rubber band around them to keep them together or place them in separate envelopes marked "Things I Need to Do" and "Things I Want to Do."

Now you will have two piles or two envelopes, simple and not so overwhelming.

It all becomes more doable having cleared the mind clutter by organizing all the things you need to do and want to do.

I suggest doing one task from the "need to do" pile first and then rewarding yourself, if possible, with something from the "want to do" pile. You can truly enjoy your time doing the things you want to do, knowing the things that need to be done are done. This approach can help keep you motivated and give you a sense of satisfaction and peace of mind.

Someone once shared the following concept with me, which I have found to be very useful in my life.

If you want to have a great day, do something you have been

putting off (from the to-do list), something for someone else (this could be either "need to do" or "want to do"), and something for yourself (most likely this is in the "want to do" pile).

The "Clear the Mind Clutter" exercise can also be done for daily, weekly, monthly, yearly, or even lifetime needs versus wants. This process can also work well for the bigger goals in life, the bucket list, if you will: having a certain experience, owning a home, taking a vacation, or expanding your education.

Feel free to toss any one-time task or desire card when completed, or, if you like, keep them in another envelope marked "Finished." Looking back at what you've accomplished from time to time will feel good and act as further motivation. By the same token, getting rid of a card that represents something you truly didn't want to do, but did anyway, can give you closure.

You can use the same method by making lists rather than using the index cards if you are a person who needs to see it all in front of you at one time, or you can spread out the cards on the table to give you a full picture of the tasks at hand. "Clear the Mind Clutter" can provide you with an easy tool to have the quality of life you wish.

### *Note to Self*
Most importantly, have fun making it work for you!

# Stop Poking the Seeds
## So You Can Reap the Harvest

Have you ever planned for an event or worked on a business plan, finding you just couldn't put it down, forever revisiting the to-do list, changing this and changing that? This is when I say, "Stop poking the seeds."

For example, take the case of one of my clients who was putting a business plan together. She was faced with what, at times, seemed like an endless process as she wrote one draft after another of her mission statement, created a new name and logo for her company, and, finally, wrote a tag line.

She sat in my office and said, "I continue to go over all aspects of the plan again and again, rewriting and editing, wanting to be sure everything is just right."

This is when I said, "Stop poking the seeds!"

I shared with her that revisiting the business plan over and over again, shifting a word here or there, is like poking the soil, checking to see if the seeds that were planted have begun to sprout.

The seeds can't begin to germinate and grow to their full potential if you keep poking at them. The farmer needs to take many things into consideration before planting the crop. He asks the questions: "What crop would produce the highest yield on that land? Is there adequate water supply? What is the pH of the soil and will there be a need for additional fertilizer? Is there additional field preparation to be done, such as picking rocks or tilling the land before planting the seeds?" Once the seeds are planted and the farmer has done all that can be done, the rest is up to Mother Nature.

We need to wait patiently for her to work her magic and stop poking and prodding the seeds we plant, otherwise we will risk over-tending them, which results in the opposite of what we had hoped. You need to trust in all you have done, just as the farmer does. You need to give your seeds time to grow.

The same held true for my client, the corporate executive, who, after much planning and implementing the appropriate steps, needed to step back and trust.

The organization of an event, such as a wedding, a birthday party, or a family or class reunion, is no different than the art of farming, from planting to harvest.

There are many areas of our life in which this can be applied. Another example might be something as simple as planning a trip: buying your ticket, making reservations, even scheduling the arrangements for transportation to the airport. There comes a time to let the event run its course.

I suggest we stop poking at the seeds we plant, allowing our ideas to germinate, knowing we have done everything to the best of our ability, and trust that the Universe will provide.

### Note to Self

Trust that the Universe will provide.

# Sorry

Let's look at the statement, "I am sorry."

How many of us seem to hear ourselves constantly saying "I'm sorry" for this or that? Before we know it, we're sorry for everything and anything that happens in our lives and the lives of everyone else around us.

How many of us have said "I'm sorry" for things that had nothing to do with us?

We often apologize for things beyond our control or that simply do not need to be apologized for. Constantly apologizing can cause our self-esteem to plummet.

Taking a good look at how and why you use the statement "I'm sorry" can be helpful. You can substitute other words that won't imply you had control over the situation in question or that you intentionally premeditated the behavior. You might really be frustrated or sad.

When someone dies, we react by saying, "I'm sorry," when what we are really feeling is sorrow. Being sad allows us to continue to have unconditional love for ourselves and others. Being sorry in this situation may imply you believe you did something wrong, and there is no self-love, no unconditional love here.

For me, it was a very small change that had a great impact on the way I thought of myself.

Not being sorry all the time opened up unconditional love for myself as well as a wonderful sense of not being responsible for others to have joy in their lives.

# Be a Duck

If you ever find yourself unhappy and feeling stuck in a situation—at work, in a relationship, or in a living arrangement that cannot be easily changed in the immediate future—I suggest you become like a duck.

Let the non-supportive words or energy of others simply roll off you like water off a duck's back.

For a good example of this, one of my female clients who had a need-to-please was living with a man who had control issues. You put the two together and it created a stressful situation for this woman. She began to have physical symptoms—heart palpitations, blood vessels breaking in the whites of her eyes, and fatigue. I call this a step-down from the emotional to the physical plane. These were the symptoms, not the cause.

She was not able to leave immediately for various reasons. However, it had become a challenge to remain under the same roof with this man.

She was not in any physical danger (if so, finding a safe place would have been top priority and being like a duck would not be a smart choice) but was in need of a way to cope with the stress until she could rectify the situation.

I suggested she become like a duck every time he had something mean to say or had a way of getting to her, which opened up old patterns from her past that made her feel like it was her fault. (Of course, no one can make us feel a certain way, we get to choose if it is true or not.)

In a follow-up call she told me, "The duck works! I just say quietly to myself, 'I am a duck, quack-quack,' and it all rolls right off my back."

Clearly this was for the short-term, until she got her ducks in a row, if you will, making the plan she needed and implementing it so that this situation was no longer an issue for her. The need to be a duck will only be a tool in the future if she finds those old patterns creeping in again.

So, in short-term, stressful situations where you are not in danger, I suggest you become like a duck and let it roll right off your back!

### Note to Self
Keep on quacking!

# Just This Simple

Many moons ago I signed on for a weeklong yoga retreat with Rodney Yee in the heart of the Rocky Mountains of Montana.

Little did I know the lifelong lessons that would come out of my time with him as my teacher.

Just as life-altering as the exercise on writing my obituary in my Polarity Training was an equally important lesson when Rodney shared with us the idea that doing the same yoga posture once a day every day for thirty days will change your life.

Imagine, just one yoga posture!

I continue to integrate this concept into many areas of my life.

One powerful way is to stop saying or thinking a prerecorded internal response that is not supportive.

It may even be something you say out loud to yourself or others on a regular basis.

For example, "Why me?" or, "Life isn't fair."

Remember that thinking is just as powerful as saying it out loud.

Be totally honest with yourself. What is the automatic response in your head?

I invite you, over the next thirty days, to embrace whatever life throws your way without getting caught up in the old message.

Erase and replace the automatic tape, statement, or way of thinking that gets in the way of feeling joy every day of your life.

If you find yourself back in the old negative thought pattern, replace it with two new positive thoughts and get on with your day.

The first positive voids out the negative while the second sets the new pattern, a new vibration, and gives more credence.

Life is just what it is, not good, not bad, just a place to learn and grow. Too often as humans, we put the spin on something that it is good or bad, right or wrong, when we could choose to step back and look at what the gift or the lesson might be in the experience.

This simple shift in thinking has the potential to create a more energetic, happier, and healthier you.

### Note to Self

One new supportive thought pattern for just thirty days will change your life.

## Gram's Pitcher

Years ago my husband's grandmother, Gram, gifted me with a beautiful, antique, white and blue pitcher that I had always admired. It wasn't fancy or overly fragile, however it was very old. She said it was from her grandmother and she wanted me to have it.

At the time we had just moved into our first home and had two small children who were less than two years apart in age. I knew if I placed that beautiful keepsake in the wrong location it might accidentally get broken. Putting it on a ledge high above the kitchen cabinets, well out of the reach of little hands, kept it safe.

Since then it has moved four times with us. Every time the pitcher has had a place high on top of the kitchen cabinets, out of the reach of anyone and less likely to be broken. I continue to treasure the gift, keeping it always in sight and never having to be concerned with its safety.

Everything we hold valuable deserves the respect that mirrors the level at which we treasure it.

As with Gram's pitcher, we have beliefs and values we hold near and dear to our hearts. When we take stock in those things we value in our life and place them in such a way that they are safe, we are not as likely to let other people's opinions and actions affect us.

We recognize that there are some individuals in our lives who do not understand, who often don't honor the essence of who we are, and thus break our spirits. They are no different than a small child who cannot understand the value or importance of an old blue and white pitcher.

So, just as with Gram's gift, remember, it is your right and responsibility to keep safe what you value.

### *Note to Self*

Honor the essence of who you are and enjoy life to its fullest!

Notes to Self

Notes to Self

### Live the Life You Want
We all have one thing in common; we live one minute
at a time. For none of us really knows when we will
breathe our last breath.

### Staying on Track
Remember to ask the question.

### Realizing the Power of Acceptance
Remember—it's better to love myself and have joy
in my life than to let the past rule the present and
take the joy from me.

### The Shredder
It's not always about me.

### Is It Good for Me?
Always take the time to listen and then
trust the answer I hear.

### Sort the Laundry
I cannot do it all at once and do it well. I will take one
pile at a time and trust the process.


### Scale of 1 to 10
When I need clarity, I will ask the question.


### Clear the Mind Clutter
Most importantly, I will have fun making it work for me!


### Stop Poking the Seeds
I trust that the Universe provides.


### Be a Duck!
I am a duck! Harmful words roll off my back.


### Just This Simple
Thinking one new supportive thought pattern for
just thirty days will change my life.


### Gram's Pitcher
I honor the essence of who I am and choose to
enjoy life to its fullest!

*MORE ABOUT THE AUTHOR*

# More About the Author:

## *What Do I Do?*

Twenty-some years in the healing arts and a part of me still dreads the question, "What do you do for a living?" It continues to bring a pause to a conversation as I try to explain. Even now I struggle to write about it in an intelligent way. I search for the words to describe exactly what it is I do and how it feels in my body so that you might understand or make sense of it.

Sometimes in a conversation, I might begin with, "I am in health care," or, "I am a teacher, speaker, and, to some, a healer." Other times, "I do energy medicine and can sense another person's energy field, simply a conduit for Spirit." I find that we often fear what we do not understand. If this is a new concept to the person I am speaking with, I find they take on the "deer in the headlights look," not sure what to say, and they become nervous and a bit uneasy around me.

I have been told, and have come to believe, that I was born with a heightened sixth sense. I have the ability to see, feel, and sense another person's physical, mental, or emotional energy at multiple levels as a healer, a conduit for Spirit. I support, activate, and restore another person's natural healing energies, which are often out of balance due to illness, injury, or life's everyday stress. In my mind, a gift such as this comes with a great deal of responsibility. I'm always respectful of others and only use it when asked.

During some sessions, I simply offer a space that is safe, one of unconditional love, validating a client. Other times, and only when asked, I give honest feedback to support clients in getting clarity and offering simple suggestions on ways to navigate a particular situation in their life. I'm simply a flashlight to help guide them.

All the formal training over the years has helped me to embrace the gift, has supported my own healing, and assisted me in developing a unique private practice firmly rooted in my formal studies. With a great deal of respect for Western medicine and its place in our healing process, I found it important to develop relationships with the medical community.

Having gained the respect of physicians who are open to the benefits of complementary therapy over the past twenty years, I have been able to support many individuals of all ages and stages in their healing process.

Kenny Rogers recorded a country western song some years back about playing the game of poker that makes references to knowing when to hold, when to fold, when to walk away and when to run.

One might say I help an individual play the game of life with simple practical tools.

I am told that I listen well while holding a space for another that allows them to be honest with themselves, giving them clarity to know when to hold, when to fold, and when to move on in life.

This is my truth. I'm clear it is my role to support and serve others.

The hope is that this book, based on simple ways of thinking, empowers readers to take actions that are in alignment with their highest good, creating more joy and happiness in their everyday lives.

## Grandmother Rita

Did you ever get a random email to attend an event? I am sure you have, perhaps one that sparked your interest or seemed like a chance to do something different with no idea of the huge impact it would have on your life?

Well I did. It came from a friend inviting me to attend an event in Kansas. She was sponsoring Grandmother Rita, whose full name is Pitka Blumenstein. She's a Yupik Elder, one of the Thirteen Indigenous Grandmothers. Grandmother Rita was coming to Kansas to share her wisdom with a small group of women, and I had an opportunity to be among them.

Since I had never heard of the Thirteen Indigenous Grandmothers from Africa, Asia, Alaska, North, South, and Central America, or their mission, I did a bit of research and found out their Council is part of a worldwide grassroots movement of prayer and action. They travel the world to visit each other's homelands, to cultivate their unified prayer for peace as ambassadors of wisdom, and to pray for our children's children.

The prayers for our children's children ran deep in my being and seemed to be a thread that connected me with the

Grandmothers immediately.

The following is a quote on their website from Grandmother Rita, the wisdom of a woman born on a fishing boat and raised in Tununak, Alaska.

*"The past is not a burden; it is a scaffold which brought us to this day. We are free to be who we are—to create our own life out of our past and out of the present. We are our ancestors. When we can heal ourselves, we also heal our ancestors, our grandmothers, our grandfathers, and our children. When we heal ourselves, we heal Mother Earth."*

—Grandmother Rita

The quote spoke right to my heart. Wow! Someone else out there thinks like I do. I booked my flight, and before I knew it, I was on my way. Upon my arrival, I was greeted by beautiful sisters of the heart, and felt an instant connection to the purpose of the weekend.

Grandmother Rita's warm spirit and healing ways instantly touched my heart as I witnessed her hold a space and do a healing session for a woman attending the weekend. She was the mother of three small children who had died in a car accident while she was driving. Talk about sad, it was just more than anyone could bear to think of what that young mother was going through.

Grandmother Rita was able to hold a space. To me, that means creating a space and place in time that is safe to be with the feelings deep within one's self with no judgment or attachment—always in alignment with the highest good. Being there for this young mother as she touched the depth of her grief, releasing the guilt, the pain, and the sadness, Grandmother Rita remained grounded and strong, yet loving and gentle. I believe I witnessed the healing power of unconditional love as Grandmother Rita offered herself up as a conduit for Spirit.

It was intense and amazing at the same time. While I was feeling for the young mother, it was as if I were watching myself work with clients in my office. The healing ritual, the way in which Grandmother Rita moved, the prayers that Spirit gifted her, all looked, sounded, and felt so familiar to me.

After lunch that day, I was privileged to sit with Grandmother Rita and her companion. I had no formal shamanic training myself, yet it was as if I had shadowed Grandmother Rita in portions of my own healing practice. They listened to me share my fears of speaking the prayers that come to me intuitively while working with clients in my office or at ceremonial sweat lodges and fire circles. So much of my work has been grounded in what has always felt like Native tradition, but my fear of offending anyone, especially Native Americans, was holding me back at some level. They both encouraged me to let the intuitive words that come from my heart be heard by others.

Later that afternoon, Grandmother Rita led our group in a prayer that was planned to take place worldwide for the healing of Mother Earth. If you can, imagine the power of people all around the globe, in different time zones, offering prayers for Mother Earth simultaneously. It resonated deep within my soul as she encouraged me to share the words out loud that seemed to come from a time long ago, those that Spirit so graciously channeled through me that day.

It is with deep gratitude I will forever hold my time with Grandmother Rita in my heart for the loving validation to be the healer that I was born to be.

## *My Sixth Sense*

Some ask me, "What do you see, feel, or hear when you work with someone? What does the client experience during a session with you?"

I often get a sensation that guides or speaks to me, suggesting what another person may have experienced, a place they are stuck, or something they may be holding onto at the physical, emotional, or energetic level. My senses, including that sixth sense, become heightened.

For example, sometimes I taste or smell the nicotine of a smoker or the effects of anesthesia post-surgery. Sometimes, like a silent movie running in my head, I can see what happened during an event in their life without them sharing the details. With someone who has experienced heartache, trauma, or abuse issues, I might feel the sadness on an emotional level, my eyes often well up with tears. Strange as it might sound, I also can get what I call a "hit." It is like someone else is speaking to me. It might be a suggested direction, or a "yes" or "no" to what they are questioning in their life. I know this sounds crazy to some. Yet I know without doubt I do not do this work alone.

Early in my career, it became very clear to me that I am a conduit for something much larger than myself. One day in session with a client, as I held a space for her, I literally felt a sensation of being ten feet tall and filled with light. At the conclusion of the session my client expressed a sense of peace at the core of her being, and then with awe shared her experience of witnessing what appeared to her to be the presence of a large angel engulfed in white light.

Supporting others in their healing is an honor and a blessing. When asked what the client feels or receives in a session, I felt it's best explained in their own words.

*TESTIMONIALS*

# Testimonials

*Cheyenne has been my teacher, inspiration, counselor, life coach, natural healer and friend for more than 25 years.*

*I was a sales executive for a major financial institution and a divorced parent raising three active sons. She helped give me the tools to use when challenges arose and to live a fulfilling, happy life as well.*

*Cheyenne helped me find peace in my heart, work with my strengths and weaknesses, find my purpose, and gain clarity. I have overcome many fears due to her guidance. It has been an honor and privilege to work with her, and I feel blessed. To know her is to love her!*

*Cheyenne presents an encyclopedia of tools for living your best life. She has always been ahead of her time with her philosophy.*

—— *Gayle Trauger*

*Cheyenne is one of few people with the gift of enlightenment. My perspective on life and its challenges is always positive after talking with her. I am fortunate to know such a wise woman and I treasure our friendship.*

—— *MJ Kelly*

*The following quote is the essence of how I feel about Cheyenne's help in dealing with a major life tragedy. Her guidance in the past has given me insights and confirmed what is in my heart to be true. She has been the arrow to point the way and prod me on.*

— *Petrona Charles*

"*In everyone's life, as sometimes happens, our inner fire goes out. It is then burst into flame by an encounter with another human being. We should all be thankful for those people who rekindle the inner spirit.*" — *Albert Schweitzer*

*Being a caretaker is a job that throws many different challenges at me. Cheyenne supplied me with many tools to face the role of caretaker, wife, and mother. After each session, I feel renewed and ready to go back and face my challenges, armed with new tools.*

— *Mary Sari*

*Working with Cheyenne I find myself grounded with more clarity and vitality to bring into my life and work.*

— *Nancy Baker, Life Coach*

*The services offered by Cheyenne have helped educate me, professionally and personally, and have offered me the ability to achieve work/life harmony.*"

— *L. Powers, Vice President of Marketing*
*Furia Rubel Communications*

*When Cheyenne Mease was introduced as special guest speaker at my first cancer-support group meeting, I was immediately taken with her positive presence, warmth, and energy. Having been thrown off kilter by my serious diagnosis and gloomy prognosis, I was grateful for the sense of relief and renewed hope that Cheyenne brought.*

*I arranged for polarity therapy sessions with Cheyenne and each one left me feeling energized, optimistic, and balanced. Determined to heal, I felt utterly confident that our work together was a significant factor in my recovery. Despite my twelve chemotherapy treatments and my surgeries, I felt strong and sure. Now, nearly fourteen years later, I am free of illness and filled with enthusiasm for life.*

*Cheyenne has also been instrumental in helping others in my family find clarity, strength, and peace of mind during periods of illness, loss, stress, and soul searching. We all hold Cheyenne in high regard and recommend her to others in need of her powerful and unique gifts.*

*—— Pamela Curtis Swallow*
*Author of books for children and teens*

*Cheyenne has a way of empowering without judging, a way of challenging without aggression, and a way of making me accountable to myself. She gave me the help I needed, which has set me on a long lasting path of change. It was more than I could have ever expected.*

*—— Paul Miller, Shigung*

*Working with Cheyenne rebalances energy in a way which allows one to be receptive to internal wisdom. Cheyenne communicates this wisdom in a caring, loving manner that creates a safe atmosphere, thereby allowing one to accept truths and possibilities.*

—— *Barbara K. Folts Psychologist*
*and Past Life Therapist*

*I have repeatedly referred personal friends and relatives to Cheyenne for both physical and emotional healing, confidently, knowing I could trust her with my loved ones. Personally, she has helped me quickly recover from major surgery, as well as find clarity and peace in stressful situations and relationships. I always breathe easier after a session with her, whether it's been face-to-face or through distance work on the phone.*

—— *D. Sarandrea*
*CEO, Harmony Clean Inc.*

# Acknowledgements

## With love and gratitude, I humbly thank the following people:

My husband, Jeff. For riding the roller coaster, all the while loving me, even when I was struggling through my early days of pain and healing.

My children, Nevada and Cody. For inspiring me to choose life.

My parents, Don and Emma. For giving me life and loving me.

My brother, Jay, and his family, my in-laws, Susie and Ralph. For being the beautiful and loving people they are in my life.

Ralph Mease. For the generous gift that was a springboard to publishing of the book.

Gina Furia Rubel. For telling me to stop listening to those who said I couldn't write and to just start writing. For believing in me.

Kelly Simcox. For always being there for me with love in her heart.

Angie Fulginiti. For believing that I could and would do it.

Lisa O'Connell. For listening to me as I read chapters to her over the phone.

Sean O'Connell. For firmly reminding me that Lisa would have wanted me to finish and not to give up when I found myself lost in the grieving process of my dear friend, his wife, Lisa.

Dr. Aurora Hill. For giving it to me straight and offering me a safe space and time to say "no" to finishing the book.

Ede Schreiner. For stepping in at just the right moment when I needed a good kick in the butt and pointing out that my voice and personality had been lost in the first edit. Almost demanding I bring me back.

Shelia Jacobs. For sharing information and thoughtful encouragement.

MJ Kelly. For a genuine interest and an honest desire for me to succeed.

LisaBeth Weber. For her willingness to read over the final edits with a fresh set of eyes.

Barb Baker. For her silent prayers to the Grandmothers and showing up when I needed help tending my medicine wheel.

Gary Straus, teacher and mentor. For the guidance to go with my strengths.

Diane Alex, Martine Bloqulaux, Amy Klaus, FreeDom Platia, Luisa Rasiej. For the supportive healing sessions over the years to keep me upright and together.

D. Freeman. For being there in many different ways, ready to open his schedule to record the audio version of the book when it was finally ready.

Shigung Paul Miller. For holding a space for me during my internal martial arts training around the ups and downs of the writing and publishing of the book and teaching me that "to quit is not an option."

Dr. Stuart H. Freedenfeld. For building the walls for my first office space and offering me access to his partners and staff who embraced my healing practice, the beginning of working with the medical community.

Dr. Joann Burke. For the many referrals over the years along with all the other physicians, therapists, chiropractors, friends, and family members who have provided me with an amazing client base that has given me the opportunity to work with so many individuals.

David Baker and Pam Swallow, accomplished published writers. For giving me their time, energy, and honest feedback from the very first mess of a manuscript with no judgment to their guidance along the way. I always felt their genuine support, be it at a wine and cheese party or sharing a meal together.

Petrona Charles. For the countless hours of revisions while teaching me the basic art of writing with the patience of a saint. She held a safe space for me to talk out some of the more difficult memories of my life, through it all reminding me to "remember, it is YOUR BOOK."

Debi Sarandrea. For being an extra set of eyes for edits, even when she was sailing in the Bahamas.

Roxanne Black (Friends Health Connection). For her gentle supportive words of wisdom from her own experience of writing and publishing her book.

Andrea Hurst. For her honesty and taking the extra care working with me on final evaluation and direction.

Bernie Siegel, MD, for graciously mentoring me when the going got tough near the end and I just wasn't sure what to do, or how to do it.

Terree Yeagle. The Moment Photography. For the book's incredible cover photograph.

## ACKNOWLEDGMENTS

Mary Skyzer. For stepping in at the 12th hour taking my collection of possible titles and bringing it all together. She nailed it!

Chanin Milnazik, friend and graphic designer. For designing an amazing cover for my book and for the copy layout, along with her honest review of the manuscript and her unwavering friendship.

Brenda Lange, my intrepid editor. For never giving up on me. She truly provided for me the very base to make my book come to life. I could not have done this without her. She took a pile of papers and sorted them out, giving some sense of order for me to make each revision. She never said no to reworking it and continues to be a stable force when it seems the seas are way too deep for me—all the while deepening our friendship.

Last but not least, each and every one of my clients. For having faith in my work and me. They all gave me a gift, a deep resource, the petri dish of learning. Without them this book would not be possible. Thank you.

I celebrate each and every one of you.

Love ~ Light
Cheyenne